A Life

Postured

In Prayer

Davronia "Val" Scarbrough

A Life Postured In Prayer

ISBN: 978-0-9995498-2-7

Published April 2020
ScarbroughED Publisher
PO Box 29515
Charlotte, NC 28229

Thank You

First, I want to thank the Father (El Elyon Most High). This book would not be possible without God the Father maker of heaven and earth, who with his tender-heart sent Jesus to reconcile "me" back to himself through the lamb that was slain before the foundations of the world. It is an absolute honor to serve Jesus Christ my Lord and Savior, the lover of my soul, the lifter of my head and the best older brother a girl could ask for. The love you showed for me Jesus over two-thousand years ago still warms my heart today, thank you for your grace. Also, I want to thank The Holy Spirit for spending precious time with me as He led me and guided me into all truths as I penned the pages of this book.

Last but surely not least, I want to "thank" & "dedicate" this book to the High Priest of my home, my husband, my best friend, my soulmate, my smile, my lover Eddie Scarbrough. I want to thank you for your patience, love and understanding during the time of writing this book. Thank you for your loving ears as I shared with you line-up-on-line of each chapter and your input and insight was invaluable. The anointing upon your life is a treasure to me and because of your love, patience and spiritual guidance I was able to complete this assignment.

Thank you, babes, for pushing me in this direction. Because it was revealed to you this was the season to release this book, I now have one more assignment completed. Eddie, you have always been my biggest cheerleader and supporter. "THANK YOU"!

Eddie, I love you and always know you are the only one to take me there, and I look forward to laboring with you until death do us part or us being raptured home together.

Book Chapters

My Journey

Make The Connection

Chosen Too Change The Atmosphere

Steady As You Go!

Don't Be Afraid of Warfare

The Enemy Can't Stop Your Yes

& Amen

Walk In Authority

Victory In Jesus

Foreword

Val Scarbrough's new book, "A Life Postured in Prayer" is a must read for every believer who desires a closer walk with God through prayer. Her love for God and the word are evident in this writing as well as her passion to pray.

James 5:16 in the Amplified bible states, "The earnest (heartfelt, continued) prayer of a righteous man makes tremendous power available [dynamic in its working]." There is tremendous power available to you as a believer when you pray. Don't doubt for a minute that God can use you to pray or that God does not hear you when your pray. Psalm 34:15 states, "the eyes of the Lord are upon the righteous and His ears are always open to your prayers." Isaiah 65:24 states, "And it shall come to pass, that before they call, I will answer; and while they are yet speaking, I will hear." Not only does God hear you when you pray, but He answers prayer.

James 5:17 goes on to say, "Elijah was a human being with a nature such as we have [with feelings, affections, and a constitution like ours]; and he prayed earnestly for it not to rain, and no rain fell on the earth for three years and six months. [I Kings 17:1.] And [then] he prayed again, and the heavens supplied rain and the land produced its crops [as usual]." Just think, Elijah was a man just like you and he earnestly prayed that it would not rain, and it did not rain. Then Elijah receive a word from God that it was about to rain again so he prayed what God said to him and it rained.

When you pray the word of God in bold confidence you will see the same kind of results; answered prayer. 1 John 5:14-15 "And this is the confidence that we have in Him, that, if we ask any thing according to His will, He heareth us: And if we know that He hears us, whatsoever we ask, we know that we have the petitions that we desired of Him."

Developing our relationship with God starts with our prayer life. We are called to be watchmen on the wall; that means to be alert and ready to pray or intercede when needed. When I think of the day and time that we are living in, we need everyone to be a watchman on the wall for our homes, communities, churches, cities and nations. Prayer should be the foundation of every Christian's life. Experiencing the promises and power of God starts with prayer. Luke 18:1 states men ought to always pray, and not to faint. We ought to always pray for all things and in all circumstances. We do not pray *for* victory. When we pray, we must pray in faith *from* the place of victory, knowing that it is already done. There are three important aspects of your life that you should pray from:

1. Praying from a place of identity (knowing who you are)
2. Praying from a place of faith (knowing it is already done)
3. Praying from a place of praise (be thankful)

You will discover all three aspects in this spirit provoking book, "A Life Posture in Prayer" by Val Scarbrough. You will also learn how to connect to God and pray from a place of victory. You will discover how to shift the atmosphere when you pray that will bring Heaven to Earth. You will read a powerful testimony that will ignite your faith to believe beyond what you can see naturally and see from God's perspective. Pastor Val has been a tremendous blessing in my life and in our church family. She has led prayer in many conferences and meetings and brought Heaven's atmosphere into the place. What a blessing to learn from someone who knows how to effectively usher in the presence of God through prayer and get results.

Apostle Cynthia Brazelton

Introduction

This book would not be in existence if Holy Spirit had not spent time with me and orchestrated my thoughts to align with heavens views of prayer and the importance of prayer. So, before I type another word I want to say, "Thank You Sir"!

My consistent prayer life has structured my life in good times and helped me to navigate through some of the worst of times in my life. Living in this culture as a believer we need to intentionally live our lives in a posture of prayer. This book derived from many teachings I have taught on prayer and my countless hours of being in prayer. I value prayer as much as I value breathing! Let me say this, we must remove our lax stance when it comes to prayer. We must stop looking at prayer as being burdensome, time-consuming, or as if it is ineffective. Prayer is our lifeline and heaven's pipeline.

The power of prayer is one of the believer's greatest weapon. I have found many believers are defeated because they do not take prayer serious enough to incorporate it in their daily regimen. Instead of taking stress as a bed partner we should rest daily in prayer. Instead of focusing on becoming prosperous at the cost of having no peace of mind, we should bathe our minds with the peace that comes with prayer. Prayer is my whoo-sah.

My prayer life is what keeps me sane and keeps me engaged with the kingdom of God (God's way of doing things).

My life of prayer is priceless. I do not know what I would do if I could not pray.

Listen, there are no gems in this earth to compare to the beauty of a life postured in prayer. I literally pray about everything. Believers think prayer has to be this long drawn out monologue expression of need and desire. No, not at all. Prayer is engaging with heaven on a constant basis like talking with a good friend, prayer is a dialog. Prayer is simply involving the father in everything concerning your life. He loves it! He takes pleasure when we involve him in our lives daily.

This book has been designed to help you develop this intimate special place with our Father and our Lord. Once you make the conscious decision to be intentional with your prayer life, your life will never be the same again. I am a witness.

Remember this as you read this book, the believer has the responsibility to inquire of the Lord, this is our role in the relationship ("men ought always pray or inquire of the Lord) (Luke 18:1-6 NKJV) with the Father.

To me one of the greatest examples of this type of dialog is shown in the life of King David. Before he went to battle, he would always inquire of the Lord "should I pursue" and each time he inquired of the Lord he would get an answer. King David literally depended on those answers for the sustainability of his life.

The bottom line my friend, God did not send us here without a connection and a weapon. Prayer is the connection and praise is our weapon!

Enjoy Your Time of Making The Connection!

Pastor Val

Enjoy!

Reading Instructions

This book has been designed to help in your daily walk with our Lord Jesus Christ and to embrace the beauty of prayer. My hope and prayer are that you make a connection so strong through prayer that your life will never be the same for the rest of your earthly life. As you read this book, I pray you develop a praying spirit and you will learn to depend on prayer just like you depend on air to breathe. You will find this book is set up for you to journal your times of prayer, so you can reflect on your prayer growth.

ENJOY!

Prayer strengthens your Relationship and dependence of the El Elyon the most HIGH God!

Prayer: To petition; to ask, as for a favor; as in application to a legislative body.3. In worship to address the Supreme Being with solemnity and reverence, with adoration, confession of sins, supplication for mercy, and thanksgiving for blessings received.

My Journey

How It All Started

I was raised in a family where prayer was always being released in the atmosphere. You never realize the foundation being built in you until life presents you with the necessity to prove your foundational footing. In my family it has always been a tradition before every road trip we would join hands and my grandmother, or someone would release a prayer of safety before the journey. Seeing this type of reverence for prayer built a love in my spirit for prayer. I would see my mothers' (I was blessed to have 2) praying, even other family members; but the person who gripped my attention with their prayer life, was my grandmother. We used to see her walking and talking, and everyone would think she was talking to herself or at least I thought she was talking to herself. Mu-dear, as I so fondly called her, many mornings, would be up early in her small kitchen cooking a delightful smelling breakfast and preparing for her daily routines would be praying and communing with our Savior. It would never fail, you would hear a shout out "Yes, Lord!". On more days than I can count, the smell from that little kitchen and her "Yes, Lord!" woke me up. Her communing with Jesus was our alarm clock.

You know as I think about it, I rarely saw my grandmother shout in church. (that is an African American term for feeling the touch of The Holy Spirit) but more times than I can recall I would see her praying in her kitchen and all of a sudden there she goes... "Yes, Lord!" and waving her hands back and forth giving God glory.

I have shared on many occasions when I do my teaching on prayer this one story regarding my grandmother's prayer life; it was the day her prayer life gripped my heart and seared a moment in time in my consciousness that changed my life forever.

(I will take a moment and share the story in its short version.) My grandmother's youngest son was most definitely her driving force to stay on her knees. That is all I will say about that. One day he was facing many years of imprisonment. On the day of his sentencing the phone rang to my grandmother's home and my mother answered and all I remembered hearing was an urgency in her voice with "What!", Ok, Ok and "thank you". She hung the phone up and recited the conversation to my grandmother and all my grandmother said is "well, we gonna' put it in God's hand". She pulled us to her bedside in a room with one single bed, a dresser, a nightstand and a lamp and we began to pray. For one hour all we did was pray and at the one hour mark the phone rang and the person on the other end said, "he has been sentenced to 3-yrs"; mind you he was facing 99-years because he was a repeat offender. That one moment in time is where I saw someone turn their face to the wall, prayed and got immediate results and it hooked me.

Little did I know a few years later I would be the one turning my face towards heaven looking for a "and suddenly" result. I want to pause here and explain what I mean about "And Suddenly". When you read the story of Paul and Silas in the book of Acts you see an "and suddenly" miracle take place as they set their hearts to pray. The bible tells us the following: **(Acts 16:26 NLT)** - *Suddenly, there was a massive earthquake, and the prison was shaken to its foundations. All the doors immediately flew open, and the chains of every prisoner fell off!* If the truth be told every believer expect an "And Suddenly" every time they pray, and I was not the exception to that same desire.

How my personal journey of prayer began isn't as flattering as the story of Paul and Silas. Even others that have mind blowing testimonies of what drew them to their knees. My prayer life did not start because of a wa-la moment and everything snapped in placed. No, my prayer life began because my life was in shambles, eighteen-years-old finding myself faced with a few major decisions that would set forth the course of my life pointed me in the direction of prayer. I mean, I had decisions before me so overwhelming, that taking my own life held just as much weight as any of the other decisions before me.

There was the decision of what college I would be attending in the fall, if any; then there was the decision, the most critical one of all, the decision which involved me trying to keep myself safe or out of the site lines of my abuser and how to keep my sanity through it all.

See, I was in a very abusive relationship and it seemed as if at any given time I might lose my life, if I did not decide to take it first. Everything around me seemed as if it was in a death cycle.

Then there was the most important decision facing me every day. The most important decision in my life at that time was the preparation of becoming a mother and how I was going to support this life that was depending on me to give them the best shot life could offer. It was a bit much, because if you want to put it into perspective, I was only eight years from ten years old facing enormous decisions with no clear course of actions before me.

My life was so overwhelmed to say the least, like I said, ending my life was not off the table of decisions.

Not to mention there was my past forever peeping its ugly head out too torment me every moment it got a chance (you have to get my first book to understand that statement).

However, thanks be-to-God for the prayers of the righteous. Without the prayers of the righteous during this period of my life I do not think I would be here sharing this book with you today.

Point. Blank. Period!

I said all of that to say this, prayer had to become the essence of my life. You may ask why would I say that prayer became the essence of my life? Because posturing my life in prayer forced suicide off my list of decisions; prayer strengthen my mind to the position of stability so I could navigate my way out of that abusive relationship. Prayer helped me to balance my thought life and approach the life I was so desperately running from. Prayer helped me to walk out of a 14-day stay on a psych ward, sane and ready to start college with optimism. Prayer helped me to see motherhood as something to live for and not be afraid of. Prayer became my posture.

I want to take a moment and look at this word "Posture" before we move further into my story. Posture is a position word. Posture can be seen or used as something negative or positive.

Posture definition: a particular way of dealing with or considering something; an approach or attitude.

This word posture was about to become my attitude and altitude. In October 1984 I gave birth to a beautiful baby girl 5.03oz at 34 weeks gestation but she was beautiful and alive. As her tiny body laid in the NICU (neonatal intensive care) jaundice, lungs not fully developed with tubs hooked to her and lying under a light to support her liver functions and as much as I wanted to be caught up in the beauty of being a new mom or how beautiful she was with that jet black hair with curly locks for days or how I was so proud to be her mother; circumstances pushed reality in my face and forced my prayer life to develop for someone else. That day I stepped into my grandmother's shoes turned my face to the wall and became an intercessor.

In an instant, I became my grandmother. Val, now it's your turn to pray for your child. 1984 was the year I opened my mouth on behalf of someone else with a fervency, a passion, pure faith and belief that I would see the goodness of the Lord in the land of the living.

The urgency I felt in my belly to fervently go to heaven on behalf of this little baby trumped all-natural senses.

All I knew, I must get a result today! The need for heaven to intervene on behalf for this little person who could not speak for herself became my driving force to pray without ceasing. She needed someone else to petition heaven on her behalf. In other words, my baby girl was depending on "my prayer life to give her a shot at life".

The bible shows us intercession and fervency get results. Let's look at the story of Jairus in a place of intercession and then I want to look at the Woman with the issue of blood to show fervency. There are three accounts of these stories, but I want to look at two of the accounts: the account from Mark 5:21-23NKJV (for Jairus) and the account from Luke 8:46-NKJV (for The Woman).

Mark 5:21-23 *21 Now when Jesus had crossed over again by boat to the other side, a great multitude gathered to Him; and He was by the sea. 22 And behold, one of the rulers of the synagogue came, Jairus by name. And when he saw Him, he fell at His feet 23 and begged Him earnestly, saying, "My little daughter lies at the point of death. Come and lay Your hands on her, that she may be healed, and she will live."* This father never accepted what he saw with his eyes, just like I did not accept what I was seeing with my eyes. Jairus went to a source and strength higher than himself. With all his authority as a ruler of the synagogue, he knew this problem, was going to take his turning his face to the wall and tapping into a source greater than his human ability. Just like myself, as I looked at my baby hooked up to all of those machines and laying in a bed with a lamp shining down on her little body tears couldn't fall, nor could I allow fear to grip my heart, so, immediately prayer flew out of my mouth. I prayed without ceasing until I saw what I had been seeing for 8-months, a healthy baby.

This is where I can relate to "The Woman" with the issue of blood as well. Luke 8:43-46 *43 Now a woman, having a flow of blood for twelve years, who had spent all her livelihood on physicians and could not be healed by any, 44 came from behind and touched the border of His garment. And immediately her flow of blood stopped. 45 And Jesus said, "Who touched Me?"*
The bible tells us when all denied it, even Peter said "Master, the multitudes throng and press You, and You say, 'Who touched Me?' Jesus said, "Somebody touched Me, for I perceived power going out from Me. "The bible tells us, and straightway or immediately the flow of blood stopped when she put a demand on "and suddenly".

The word tells us the "effectual fervent" prayers of the righteous avails much or I like to say it like this "It avails an "and suddenly". The word **_effectual_** means: successful in producing a desired or intended result and **_fervent_** means: having or displaying a passionate intensity.

You know I believe when Jairus left his house he was walking and talking to the father, just like my grandmother would do in that kitchen. I can see him walking a dusty road passionately pressing into heaven or drawing out of the well of "and suddenly".

Child of God, there are some situations we will face in life that the only thing that will satisfy what is at hand, is an "and suddenly".

Here I want to interject something that is especially important. Never allow one victory to make you numb to greater victories.

Which brings me to the completion of my foundation of *"A Life Postured In Prayer"*.

August 1986 I gave birth to another beautiful baby girl 7.14oz., she had a head full of curly locks like her sister, she didn't need anyone to spank her bottom to clear her lungs, because she opened her mouth the moment she completed her long journey through the birth canal and the world was fully aware she was here. There was no mistake this was my fighter and she proved that ten hours into her life outside of the womb. (Let me make something clear "they" both are fighters)

My youngest child was born with an Omphalocele (intestine outside of the abdomen - a hole in the middle of her stomach). Again, I did not have time to focus on being happy and excited about how beautiful she was because I immediately became an intercessor for the second child God had entrusted to my hands. Waiting for her to open those big beautiful eyes after emergency surgery and to hear that cry again seemed like a lifetime. What the doctors said would be 18-24 hours before I could see her, God proved man wrong once again, and ten hours later she opened her mouth to let the world know "I am here and hungry, where is my mom?"

"Pause": You would definitely have to know my youngest to fully understand that statement. One thing I quickly realized during the time of praying for my babies, is, the prayers of a mother truly can determine life or death for her children. Better yet, your prayers can determine life or death for you. I like to say it like this, what

are you going to do now life is forcing you to make a prayer decision? Are you going to pray or are you going to paste? Our outcome is determined by our P-choices. I know you may be asking what are P-choices? It's when you either Pray, Paste the floor or Ponder (deliberate/mull over) a situation.

My life postured in prayer started because someone sparked a thirst in me to see heaven move in any situation, my P-choice was to pray. I am so grateful and thankful for the day the Father positioned me in that little bedroom at my grandmother's house and gave me a glimpse of the power of prayer. My life has never been the same since that day.

Remember, I showed you the meaning of posture. Also, I said it is an attitude. Well just know, my "Life Postured In Prayer" is an attitude and my altitude. The reason I say that is because I know, I have seen and I am confident there is nothing, I mean No-Thing to hard for God.

Make The Connection

Being Connected

Prayer is a beautiful and powerful expression of our total dependence on God. However, many today seem to wonder whether their prayers are being heard. When clearly if you call, he will answer (never doubt that). Jesus said it like this, "Father I know you hear me every time I pray". The bible also tells us in 1 John 4:7 *"As Jesus is, so are we in this world"*. So if Jesus declared "Father I know you hear me every time I pray" we have to have that same assurance; every time we commune with Him, every time we call out to him, He hears us and is ready to answer my sincere petition brought to the throne of Grace.

As a believer, a strong prayer life indicates to the world our connection to heaven and our total dependence on the Father. Our connection to heaven is a statement to this world, the Father will arrange things in the earth realm to move and produce in my favor. When our petitions are faith filled, there is an assurance every time we pray, we expect an answer to what have laid before our Father.

There is a sad, mind boggling statistic over 70% of believers don't believe God hears their prayers, they have lost the sincere desire to seek help from Him or they just feel as if there are other things that can assist with God's Yes & Amen for their lives.

If you are sitting there like I was when I read that stat, right now your mouth is wide open in disbelief of this unfortunate truth.

I believe to reduce that stat listed above, a blood bought believer making-the-connection with heaven is the key to total reliance and belief in what we say. Our convictions or our reliance on heaven must originate from the following thought pattern and belief system:

1. We must have an absolute unprecedented desire to see heaven move in the earth. Matthew 6:10 _"thy kingdom come; thy will be done in earth as it is in heaven"_ must be the strongest desire when we open our mouths to pray.

We have to be assured in our hearts there is a will for our lives that has been established in heaven and it is the Father's delight that it manifests here in the earth. This must be a conviction without any reservation. David puts it like this **(Psalms 27:14 NIV)** _I remain confident of this: I will see the goodness of the Lord in the land of the living. Wait for the Lord; be strong and take heart and wait for the Lord_

2. As a believer you have to be assured that He is concerned about your life and his priority is always you! Making-the-connection to heaven is like making a connection with any earthly relationship.

With earthly relationships when you know someone intimately, no one can tell you about who that person is and what they bring to the table; why, because you know them intimately. When you posture your life in prayer or make-the-connection to heaven, you have declared the relationship is solid and I know God intimately and innately. The more we converse and spend time with heaven the better the conversations becomes and the more frequently we will want to converse with heaven. The more we make-the-connection with heaven the greater our relationship flourishes and our belief in the Father's ability strengthens.

As a parallel, I will say again, the more confident we are in our earthly relationships, the better these relationships are. The stronger our earthly relationships are the better the chance our conversations will have a positive impact in the connection. Think about it when someone makes you feel positive it trickles down to your everyday interactions. Making-the-connection with heaven is no different.

Moses and Daniel are great examples of people that showed what and how a strong prayer life brings physical manifestation and how their prayer life built a relationship with God that we gladly put on display today.

These men were both reverent, obedient, and connected to the Father through their prayer life and please let us not forget about Elijah's prayer life. (Which I find absolutely amazing)

It would take another book to tell of his amazing stories and the power exhibited in the earth realm through his connecting to God through prayer. There is nothing like the amazing feeling of connecting to our savior Jesus Christ in prayer. Like the old saints use to say, "Jesus is on the mainline call him up and tell what you want!" Halleluiah!

Being connected and knowing you are connected to heaven through your prayer life invokes this intimacy that will push words out of your mouth like "Father, I know you hear me every time I pray". Both Moses and Daniel gained tremendous strength from their relationship in prayer and had great influence with the Father through their prayer connection. Let me say again, MAKE THE CONNECTION! Making your heaven-connection through intentional prayer is how you solidify your voice print in the heavenlies. (Luke 18:1-2 NKJV) Remember in the story in Luke 18 states "The widow woman **_continually_** made her request known". What was she doing? Solidifying her voice print; believe it or not she was developing a relationship and a connection. Why did Jesus do this thing call praying so often? Because He understood the bonus/benefits of "The Connection". Listen, Jesus, Moses, Daniel, Elijah and the Widow woman all recognized, all wisdom and provisions for life were given by the Father and when there is a need, them making their request known is what will prove "whose I am and who I am." Shout right now "I Am Connected". Know this, every devil in hell is banking on you discounting, forfeiting and abandoning your connection.

Devils understand this fact, man's connection to heaven is the most powerful thing on the planet. So, he wants us to become so moved by situations and circumstances we do not create a "voice print" in heaven through prayer.

Beloved, please hear me, your prayer life is the lifeline to your walk/pilgrimage here in the earth. Make the connection by praying with and in faith, by never allowing the enemy to shut your mouth while bashing your head and please never-ever discount the power of "_**A Life Postured in Prayer**_". Believe it or not God is depending on your prayer life; why, because heaven has miracle, signs and wonders waiting to be released but heaven depends on our prayers to make the request known. So, my friend I encourage to "Make The Connection"!

I want to give you a few ideas on customizing your connection.

Customize Your Prayer Time

1. **Make room for prayer in your life**

   To make room for prayer you must open your heart to pray at any given time.

2. **Make a list of things you desire to see happen in your time of prayer**

   Your list during prayer is simply writing the vision and making it plain. Your list is symbolic to going before the Lord continually and specific. Let me stop here and say, "don't get lost in the moment". Prayer can get so good and his presence can become so overwhelming sweet that you can miss the opportunity to pray specifically. Yes, he knows our thoughts before we speak them; however, you have a part to play in prayer and that is releasing the petition.

3. Work through distractions

Remember this, the devil hates your prayer life and the longer he can keep you on mute, the longer he can cause havoc in your life; the longer he keeps you distracted the longer he keeps you defeated. Defy the distractions and make them insignificant. Do not allow distractions to exhaust you to the point you cannot pray. Distractions causes one to think there is no value in prayer; consequently, you will put off praying until there is a more perfect time to pray (such a misnomer). This is one of the strongest weapons the enemy uses against the believer, "distractions".

Father my prayer is:

_____

_____

_____

_____

_____

_____

_____

_____

_____

_____

_____

_____

_____

Chosen Too Change the Atmosphere

"The Woman"

Luke 7:36-50

A *Life Postured in Prayer* is a life submitted to being used in any situation to show forth the power, goodness, mercy, and grace of God. This is absolutely one of my favorite stories in the bible. I call her the woman who distributed change! This passage of scripture is about "*A Life Postured In Prayer*". I see a woman who demonstrated "A Life Postured In Prayer" at a great level. Here in this story we actually see two postures being displayed: the posture of "chosen" and the posture of "change". As believers we have to open our eyes and see the significance of our "posture". Let's talk about the posture of "chosen".

Chosen is absolutely a privilege word. Chosen signifies our connection to heaven and our position. Chosen also shows others our relationship with Jesus and how it holds a superlative place in our lives. Brace yourself, chosen communicates to the world "my relationship with Jesus is being put on display". This woman was "chosen". Her behind scene relationship was being put on display for all to see.

Child of God, as we set our hearts to see the power of God move in situations and circumstances there is a posture-shift that must take place. This woman in (Luke 7:36-50 NKJV) was hand-picked to walk into a room of people and distribute "change". Her posture delivered a message from heaven that turned a dinner party conversation into a conversion service.

Let me say this my friend, that is what pure intercession looks like. Yes, this may have started out as an upper echelon party orchestrated in the flesh, but we have been chosen to bring heaven into mundane places. This was a dinner party with a cold climate and heaven used this woman to change the temperature of the room. The scripture which is the most powerful to me in this whole story is (Luke 7:38 NLT), because it stated, *38 Then she knelt behind him at his feet, weeping. Her tears fell on his feet, and she wiped them off with her hair. Then she kept kissing his feet and putting perfume on them.*

This is what I want you to see, she changed her posture which change their perception. I do hope you see this was a divine set-up from heaven. Everything in this scripture screams "connection and prayer". The prayer out of this woman's belly was so powerful it became an illustrated sermon. Glory! (Again, I could write another book just on that scripture; however, let's move on) The second posture we see in this story is that of "Change". Now "change" itself has two components to it: a sound and a look. This story may seem as if it is taking us to the destination of the woman being in a desperate need of a "change" and she was; however, true intercessors first go to God about themselves; because true intercessors are more concerned with being a pure vessel for the assignment at hand than being on display. This is one thing a true intercessor knows and say daily "yes, I am chosen to change atmospheres; however, I definitely find it more valuable to have a pure relationship with Jesus as the central part of my existence". So, we cry out daily, "Give me a clean heart". (Psalms 24:4 NKJV)

Remember I just stated that "change" has a look? Luke 7:38 talks about her kneeling. In prayer there must be a place of submission. I know the question lingering in your mind, what if I am not in a place where I can physically kneel? Kneeling is a physical and spiritual act. You can physically kneel, or you can spiritually kneel by humbling your heart. Both are places of submission and both have a look.

In the book of (Isaiah 6: 8 NKJV) the Father ask this question to Isaiah, *"Who shall I send? Who will go for us? Isaiah said, "Here I Am".* Yielding himself to the assignment God had placed before him was an indication he was willing to be chosen to change atmospheres. When you are chosen, you must be willing to go into places that will require the "Atmosphere to be Changed" and you cannot be timid when you go in. I will say this, when your *Life Is Postured In Prayer* many assignments will be cold and carnal(like that dinner party), and may seem impenetrable but knowing you have been called for "such a time as this" pushes one to the kneeling place.

Knowing you have been called to change the temperature in rooms strengthens your prayer life, because you understand where the true power comes from. Your *Life Postured In Prayer* isn't just for you, it's for others as well. We could talk about Esther right here, but we will move on.

Being "Chosen Too Change The Atmosphere" is what *"A Life Postured In Prayer"* is all about. Our prayer life should be making marks that will be remembered for generations to come.

Remember, I told you earlier in this chapter this is one of my favorite stories, there is sadness to this story as well. Until this woman walked into the room there were people at the dinner table with a muted prayer life, a form of godliness and no desire to see "change" take place in their mundane lives.

They thought they were simply fine. It took a woman, who I believe had a prayer life before she walked into the room; because there are just certain postures a prayer life reveals. A person with a prayer life changes the topics at dinner parties and shift the focus to "We all need a Savior". Prayer is about connecting to a greater source than our limited ability, knowledge and understanding of heaven.

Another example of "Chosen Too Change The Atmosphere is when Jesus asked, "Who do men say I am"? In other words, I hear Jesus saying this...What does your connection to heaven reveal to you about me? In your prayer time Peter "what did you hear heaven say about me"?

You know over the years we would give Peter somewhat a hard time because he denied Jesus amid pressure; however, Peter never denied him in prayer. Therefore, Jesus could say "Upon this rock I will build my church" and Peter tapping into prayer, making the connection to heaven caused him to be filled with the Holy Spirit and have the first mega church post Jesus. Glory!

When you are chosen to change the atmosphere everything around you will shift. The places you will go, the people you will encounter, and the instructions you will hear.

I want to point out a few things about intercession.

Intercession

- **Intercession"** is not God trying to teach you something; but it's God's way of showing you what you have on the inside of you that represents "being made in His likeness". You can speak to darkness and say "let there be light".
- **"Intercession"** shows the enemy the Father's likeness downloaded in his children to **command, demand, and expand** at any time.
- **Intercession** is an indication of the time you have spent with God before the battle.
- **Intercession** is targeted prayer (you become a sniper in the spirit you do not pray amiss)
- **Intercession –** is understanding and using the authority given to us through the redemptive work of Jesus Christ. It is called Exousia. (**Exousia**- operates by exercising God-given rights. It's positional power which causes both angels and demons to move. Exousia operates often by the Spoken Word.)

Remember, we have been chosen to change the atmosphere. Take a moment and ask Jesus who have you called me to intercede for today? Or Ask him what atmosphere you have been called to change; He will show you. Then yield and say "Here I Am" send me.

Steady As You Go!

Set Your Face

I know we covered Isaiah 6: 8 in the last chapter where the Father asked the question to Isaiah, "Who can I send? Who will go for us? Isaiah said, "Here I Am". This is the most powerful statement any believer can make to the father, "Here I Am"! Your "Here I Am" is going to take you having a steady mind, a fix heart, and a face set like flint. Your "Here I Am" takes a strength to posture your life in prayer. Steady as you go literally communicates to others, I will remain unchanging, collected, and relentless in my prayer life.

Let us examine a man that was unchanging in his prayer life. I would even go as far as saying rigid in his prayer life. This man happens to be one of my favorite people in the old testament, his name is Ezekiel. I was so fascinated with him that the book of Ezekiel is the first book in the bible I read in its entirety. This man's life was truly postured in prayer, even though he was surrounded by people that did not care much for prayer.

His assignment was one that seemed impenetrable, but he was steady and unmoved by those things and people around him. When I say steady as you go, I am saying do not look to the left nor right just keep praying. I wanna pause here and say this "today prayer is a lost art" and the sad thing is, because we are living in an age of intellect many people don't see the need or significance in having an effectual prayer life. Just like in the days of Ezekiel. Let us explore what was going on during the days of Ezekiel and see if there are any similarities to our times.

First thing to recognize is this man-of-God lived during the time of International upheaval (sound familiar). Secondly, Ezekiel lived during a time when the relationship between God in his children was strained, because many people did not worship God with a pure heart, and they had many idols (sound familiar). Thirdly, God used Ezekiel to act out a prophetic imagery of what he was hearing in prayer. Therefore, God used his faithfulness or steady life of prayer to deliver to his people heart-wrenching words of judgment. Let me say this, I believe that God is going to use those who are willing to pray without flinching in these last days to deliver messages that will go against the "culture" but will set many free! Amen!

Please do not misunderstand me. Yes, God loves his people and sent Jesus so that grace would much more abound where sin abounds; however, God is still warning his people through those that are on their face in prayer. By revealing to them there are demonic devices that have come to kill, steal, and destroy the believer's connection to heaven. The devil is after your prayer life!

Never second guest that!

In Ezekiel 3:7-9(NLT) the Father tells Ezekiel a couple of things. First, he tells him "I am going to "set" you" and secondly, he tells him "you have to allow my words to sink deep into your heart" because you will be faced with challengers that will come to oppose your prayer life. Let us unpack what the Father was saying to Ezekiel. Look at this word "set". Set means: to place (oneself) in a position to start running in a race: to appoint or assign to an office or duty: to furnish as a pattern or model: to cause to assume a specified posture or position.

That is so good to me! When we set our face like flint, we are communicating to everyone the following: I have started a race, I have accepted an appointment, and I am here to model what a life looks like postured in prayer.

My friend I hope you see why your "Here I Am" means so much to the Father. When we say, "Here I am", you and I give him legal rights to operate in the earth realm, but he can't operate in the earth if we aren't set or steady in our position of prayer. Just think, the children of Israel's whole message system during that time was determined by a man that was "Set". My question to you is "whose life right now is hinged upon you being "Set"".

I know for myself, there have been many assignments the Lord would "set" me on and I know for sure if I had not "set" my face like flint to hear what heaven was saying about the situation, death would have overtaken the situation and Victory would not have been the outcome. No, I am not saying I am God, but when your life is postured in prayer you must be assured of one thing, I am the legal gateway between heaven and earth (never let anyone make you feel shame of that fact; you are who you are by the Grace of God). **"Pause"**: I only stop to say the above-referenced statement because for many of years others would try and shame me because of my boldness in my position as an Intercessor.

Heaven is depending on us being "Set"!

For those of you that know me, know I love testimonies, as I know my testimonies puts heaven on display. So here goes.

Testimony: In 1994 my husband was facing a life-changing situation. He was facing 26-years of prison time. (You will have to hear him give his full story. It is absolutely beautiful. Anyway, we were due in court the 26th day of October to hear his fate. I said, "babe we are going too fast and pray for 3-days". We arrived at the courthouse and on the front steps we grabbed each other's hand and I began to pray and release the word of the Lord over the situation (In Faith) with full dependence of heaven being on display that day. Well, we went into the courtroom and we were in there less than 20-mins (the shortest time we had ever been in court) the Judge reviewed the things presented and he said, "Mr. Scarbrough go and have a good life"! Whatchu' say! Look at God! Glory!!! You have to "set" yourself in the midst of a hostile environment believing He hears you every time you pray.

My husband's lawyer said you had someone looking out for you. Yes, we did! Through prayer and faith, we looked for "heaven to be on display" that day and heaven never disappoints. I just know you must be steady as you go, and you cannot allow signs and symptoms to trip up your prayer life.

Let's get back to Ezekiel. Ezekiel was called to pray for people in exile. No, we are not in a physical exile but there are many in the body of Christ that are in places of spiritual exile. Depression is a place of exile. Infirmity is a place of exile. Alcoholism is a place of exile. Disappointment is a place of exile. Poverty is a place of exile. Low self-esteem is a place of exile. Addictions are a place of exile. When we do not understand our inheritance through Jesus it places us in exile. Do you see where the list could go on and on?

I want to take a rabbit trail here and deal with the place of exile called cancer. One night I went to have dinner with The Holy Spirit, yes, I take moments to go and just converse with The Holy Spirit and my husband gladly allows us to go on dates, lol. Gotta, love a man like that!

Moving right on. Well this fall evening on my date with The Holy Spirit I asked, "what is going on in the earth with this infirmity call cancer?" Why does it seem the more research being put towards this horrible disease; I mean billions of dollars are being spent to build more beautiful facilities, yet it seems more people are being diagnosed with this horrendous disease? He said to me, because the earth is making more room for this god to exist and function in the earth.

Please know I am grateful for every center that is in the earth that gives treatments to assist many people to live a long life. Jesus placed those research centers here for his children and I am eternally grateful for those men and women and their sincere dedication for all they do for others.

However, think about it, we are building temples for a god to live unrestricted. **SELAH** Remember, every name that is name is under the name of Jesus according to **Ephesians 1:21-22 NLT** *(v.21 Now he is far above any ruler or authority or power or leader or anything else—not only in this world but also in the world to* come *v.22 God has put all things under the authority of Christ and has made him head over all things for the benefit of the church.*).

So back to my date with The Holy Spirit. He said "Val because the earth has made cancer a god and when man (not gender) hear the very word cancer they allow an overwhelming fear and disappointment to overtake their hearts which sends many into exile.

The Holy Spirit said to me "so when the enemy throws signs and symptoms to my children it's hard for them to "set" themselves" because they have allowed this god(cancer) to exile in the land of "no hope". What I love about Ezekiel he did not allow exile to move him from being "set" and steady in his prayer life.

The Holy Spirit said, the word says, "if you humble yourself and pray", there is so much meat in the <u>humble</u> part of that scripture. Listen, humble does not mean that you act lowly, but this humble refers to us humbling ourselves under the <u>power of the word</u> and praying from a place of being secure in our <u>rights</u> as a blood bought believer. Glory!!

I said to The Holy Spirit, "so we have made cancer a god?", he said "yes". He said, the word says, "every name that is name is under the name of Jesus". Not everything that is named "IS GOING" to be under" the name of Jesus. No! "IT IS" under the name of Jesus!

Meaning everything that tries to have authority over you or put you in exile must come subject to your protection by and through Jesus Christ.

I know some beautiful believers that have gone home to be with the Lord, and they didn't do anything wrong, they loved the Lord and were true believers in Jesus; yet, this place of exile overshadowed their legal right to healing.

My point is, as a believer you must "set" your face like flint and be steady in prayer! Child of God it was a reason God told Ezekiel to "set" his face. You wanna know why; because as sure as I am talking to you via this book, signs and symptoms are going to come and the path to exile will present itself to you in some shape, form or fashion. Do not willingly go into exile.

Just know, it is the enemy's pleasure to put God's people in exile. It gives him pleasure when we do not humble ourselves to the word that states "By His Stripes We Are Healed"! The devil knows the power of us humbling ourselves to and under the word of God. He literally banks on us not being "set" in the word or postured in prayer.

My friend, I encourage you to be steadfast, immovable and "set" when it comes to your prayer life. The scripture states, "the effectual, fervent prayers of the righteous avails much"; which is simply admonishing us to "set our face like flint" and "steady as you go"!

When you do this, you will continue to develop a life that is postured in prayer.

Don't Be Afraid Of Warfare

Your Prayer Life Draws Warfare

I love our description from the mouth of God. We are called lions, eagles, warriors, soldiers, conquerors, war club (Jeremiah 51:20 NLT) and even given the description of a bear (2 Samuel 17:8 NLT). Know this, we the children of God, we were designed for war! In the book of Isaiah 6: 8 the Father ask this question to Isaiah, he states "Who can I send? Who will go for us? With that being said, you do know heaven is always looking for a few good warriors.

God and the heavenly host will never back away from a fight. So many believers take the easy road to Victory; (I know, there is nothing like a sweat less victory) however, there is nothing like a good ole' fight in the spirit. You are probably saying "What!" Pastor Val? Yep, there is nothing like standing in the authority of the Lord Jesus Christ in the earth realm.

Before we go any further let's establish something. Prayer alone is spiritual warfare. Yes, there are different levels of spiritual warfare but please know the moment you open your mouth to release a petition, make a declaration, intercede, or just cover your life through prayer, you have entered a spiritual fight.

Let's look at some examples of spiritual warfare. We have to start with my man Daniel, and I will give a short version so we can move along. Daniel was sensitive to things that were about to happen in his country and so he went into prayer. Daniel 10. For 21-days or 3-weeks he laid in warfare in prayer until the answer came. My point for pinpointing this story is, he did not back away from the battle of prayer. His consistency in prayer assisted the heavenly host break through warfare that was going on in the heavens.

Now the other example I want to lay out before us is Jesus and the Centurion. One thing that you must establish in your heart in warfare is, there is "No Distance" in the spirit. None!

I love this story. The centurion soldier understood the concept of 0-distance in the spirit, no lag time. Jesus sending the word to his servant represented the same as Jesus being in the room with the servant and the Centurion solider understood this concept. The Centurion solider introduced space travel to the world. Glory!! Before his mentioning of sending the word or introducing the concept of "no distance" - "no lag time" in the spirit, people thought there had to be contact for the manifestation to take place. The centurion soldier understood prayer supersedes, cell phones, facetime, in boxing, texting, or FedEx. Prayer is right now, for right now! Glory!

So many times, we think we must be in the presence of someone to pray an affective and effective prayer. No, this is not the case in the spirit. You can be in New York and someone can be in Paris and God will place a person in your spirit and tell you specifically what to pray for and how to pray for them. Prayer has the power to transcends time, space, and natural laws.

Prayer is an ever-moving frequency(carrier) in the spirit. Let me put it like this, prayer is our spiritual "courier service" from earth to heaven and heaven to earth. I know what you are thinking, heaven to earth, yes, heaven to earth.

We have love ones in heaven praying on our behalf right now, saints that have finished their earthly course but not the eternal course. Those saints are praying and asking for things on our behalf as we continue our earthly journey. So, when their prayers are answered on our behalf, in other words when they receive a "Yes" for us the yes then has to be released out of heaven into earth. Prayer is the courier service of heaven and there is "no distance" in the spirit.

Remember the scripture in Matthew 16:19 NKJV tells us, *whatever we bind on earth will be bound in heaven and what is loose in earth will be loosed in heaven*. Let us talk about the above-referenced scripture as it relates to immediate results or distance in the spirit. I want to focus on the words <u>bind</u> and <u>loose</u>. Those two words are military terms. Those two words are words used to describe authority. Per the original Jewish meaning of these two words, they are authoritative words. Bind & Loose means to **<u>forbid by an indisputable authority or to permit by an indisputable authority.</u>** With that knowledge, you now see why the word in Proverbs 18:21NKJV tells us *"life and death" are in the power (the indisputable authority) of your tongue*.

Therefore, the enemy banks on you being afraid of warfare, he is banking on you not understanding spiritual warfare and he is banking on you keeping your mouth closed during the time of spiritual warfare. I have found over the years many believers forget the word in

(Luke 10:19 NLT); *I have given you the power(authority) to trample on snakes and scorpions and to overcome all the power of the enemy; nothing will injure you.* Listen my friend, we are not defenseless. So, there is no reason for any believer to back away from spiritual warfare.

If you do not get anything else from this book than this one thing; remember, always know scripturally laced (word) prayers are weaponized truths that the devil hates for the believer to connect too and release.

I want to pause here and say something that may seem elementary, seeing that you are reading a Christian based book, but it must be said.

IT'S A SELAH MOMENT:

"Take the word of God seriously, download it in your spirit, write it on the tablets of your heart, and never think you can overeat the word of God". Obesity in the spirit has never killed anyone!

My friend spiritual battles are not, let me repeat, are not won outside of being fortified with the word of God. The greatest example of this is Jesus. In Matthew 4. Jesus was led up into the mountains by the Holy Spirit, to be tempted. I like to read it like this; Jesus was led up into the mountain to test what he had engrafted upon his heart. (to become grafted and begin functioning normally)

I can hear the thoughts of some of you. Pastor Val, I think you may be wrong about that, after all he was Jesus, he did come from heaven, and he was the word. Well, I am here to inform you that Jesus had to engraft the word upon his heart as it is written here in the earth realm through the prophets of old, so that he would not operate outside of the lines that were put in place in the earth to govern man. Remember, even though he was divinity, in the earth He operated in his humanity. The devil only operates from this place of humanity, the sense realm, the human knowledge realm; so, Jesus had to engraft the word upon his heart as it is written here in the earth. Just like you and I Jesus had to know the word! If you noticed in Matthew 4 the devil did not use or say anything that had not been revealed to man through a written form and he will always try to war against us on "what has been written". Truth be told, he is spiritually bankrupt and has no other revelation other than what is been written. Unlike you and I, we have been given Logos & Rhema, so he comes with the same scriptures to throw us off our game betting on us not knowing the "written word". Therefore, we must know the word and the word must be spirit life to us! Remember, he is banking on us punkin' down or being thrown off by his limited knowledge of the word. Child of God do not be afraid of spiritual warfare because you have authority, logos and rhema word living on the inside of you...point-blank-period. The devil is operating off old manna. In fact, he is operating his kingdom off an old rejected anointing, remember, he "was" the anointed cherub but no longer.

As I close this chapter, I want to share my personal feelings on "spiritual warfare". There have been many of times Jesus has asked me to stand in the gap for others in this place of warfare and some of the assignments have seemed overwhelmingly challenging, at least if I gave much thought to them, especially from a human standpoint. To be honest, I did not feel capable. However, every time He would and does assure me, you have my word on the inside of you and you know my voice.

My assignments have ranged from; walking people from full blown aides to health, speaking to cancer and commanding it to dry up & die, mental breakdowns to stability, from infertility to production, from commanding evil spirits to vacate homes, down to even warring on behalf of my own body and my husband's body.

Let's set the record straight...NO, I would never take the Glory from God because without the covering of the blood, the wisdom of God, the finish work of Jesus and The Holy Spirit guidance I would not have courage to fight spiritually. I am fully aware of where my help comes from.

However, I take the word of God seriously and I believe everything in the word (from the table of contents to maps) and I believe this is what has fortified me during the times of warfare. So, I close this chapter, saying "my friend, don't be afraid of spiritual warfare, but be prepared for spiritual warfare!"

Gird yourself up children of God and LET'S GO!!

The Enemy Can't Stop Your Yes & Amen

Our Yes & Amen

Remember in the last chapter I talked about Daniel, well, let us continue that subject, but I am going to infuse a few more people into the conversation. We are going to look at Esther and Hanna. When your **Life Is Postured In Prayer** your expectation every time you pray is, "yes". Just think about it, no one goes to God in prayer expecting anything other than, a yes. "News Flash", the enemy knows this and that's why he fights so hard to hold up your "yes". I remember one day I was in prayer and The Holy Spirit said to me "Val you know why the enemy tries to hold up your yes?" I said, "no" and he said, "because he thinks if he holds it up you will become tired, despondent, weary, and walk away from your "yes". I thought at that moment, so, that's why you say in Luke 18 "men/women ought always to pray and not FAINT". My friend, he is trying to get you to walk away from your "yes". I speak to you today and say... "STAND STRONG" you are wearing that devil out with your prayer life.

Ok back to Daniel and I am going to "Valnize" the scripture and let you investigate my train of thought when I throw myself into scripture, so, here -goes: (Daniel 10:1-12).

Let's look at *Daniel 10:1-12 NLT. (Verse 2.) Daniel tells us he mourned(prayed) for 3-weeks about the same thing. Not wavering, nor looking at the time, nor did he pay attention to the conditions. (Verse 3.) is where he gets real, he said "listen, I didn't go to Longhorn, Ruth Chris, Cracker Barrel and I gave no thought to any pleasures. Basically, Daniel was ashy for 3-whole weeks. (Humm,*

Jesus I ask you never to put me on an assignment like that)
Moving on, (Verse 7.) I have been so tapped into heaven through
intentional prayer that I can be standing in a crowd and see what
they are unable to see. People around me may be able to feel
heavens presence but I can see what they feel. (Verse 9.) I am now
able to hear on behalf of others. (Verse 10.) my prayer life has now
placed me in a position to feel the touch of heaven (Verse 11) My
prayer life has received recognition in heaven and trust in heaven
(Glory!!) My favorite part is (Verse 12.) Since you open your mouth
and heart to gain an understanding of earthly things from a
heavenly perspective or since the first day you expected a "yes" the
"my yes" was released.

In this whole monologue the angel was simply saying a war was
ensued over your "yes" and the holdup was to tire you out. I want
you to know the enemy wants us all to get so tired of praying that
we become bored in pursuing our yes. Child of God keep
praying!

On to Esther. Esther's "yes" came with a few things. It came with
promotion/authority, it came with wisdom, and it came with
developing a life of intercession. Over the years what I have come
to realize is that as an intercessor the enemy really wants you to
become <u>discouraged</u>. There is a spirit of discouragement and this
spirit has one assignment and that is to affect your next
assignment. Remember, the word of God tells us "Hope deferred
makes the heart sick". So, what it does, he tries to wreck or steal
our "yes" in the spirit(heavenlies) so we can never see the
manifestation in the earth of what we prayed for and our hearts

become discouraged and we walk away from all of our yes'. (Lord Help Us)

You know many people look at Esther's assignment and think light-hearted of it because the bible tells us she only prayed three-days. However, to carry a nation for three-days can seem like a lifetime when you are praying. See in those three-days she could have become discouraged and stopped praying. She could have lost the expectation of a "yes" and stop praying. She could have become resolute in her heart that we are going to be annihilate and started the preparation of death and died on her "yes". You best believe the enemy was counting on her walking away from her "yes".

My friend when we go to God, we must believe that He is and there is no situation standing in front of us that He is not ready to dissolve with a "Yes".

So, do not walk away from your petitions. Do not get weary in your waiting period. Keep praying because our prayers assist the courier in getting through. Remember, we talked about Daniel earlier in this chapter. Well this is what was said about his wait time.

The angel said, "I was being held up by the prince of the air and I had to call for back-up". Daniel's continuing to pray assisted in bringing in back-up. So, my friend, keep praying!

Last, but not least, Hannah. There is so much I can say about her; however, what stands out to me in her story is how her prayer looked strange in the house of the Lord. I can so relate. Over the years, I have had people to tell me directly and indirectly "It doesn't take all of that" or prayer doesn't have to be expressive to be effective". True, but mine is.

One thing I am assured of, I know what and how I feel when I am communicating & connecting with heaven, I know how intercession feels pulling out of my belly, I know how I feel when deep is crying out to deep. So, I understand Hannah. For years and even now when I pray, I get so involved in releasing my petitions into heaven. I mean, I feel it in every part of my being. (I am an intense prayer warrior). I engulf myself into prayer and for years I knew, no one had to tell me, it looked strange to some, but I keep praying. The one thing The Holy Spirit showed me about Hannah is, she felt her "yes"! She knew inside of her, her Yes was in battle. You see Samuel could not just come through any woman. His mother had to be a true intercessor. Why? Because the bible tells us "none of his words" fell to the ground. I believe Hannah's prayer that day laid a foundation for her son's words to never fall. GLORY!! You do know, you, as an intercessor can lay foundations in the heavens that can affect outcomes in the earth. From the outward appearance it looked as if Hannah was begging and pleading for a son. I believe Hannah's pray went something like this:

Father, I see what you have in me and everyone around thinks I am barren, but I feel life in me every time my husband touches me. I feel greatness being birthed out of me. Help me manifest what I see, give me strength to look pass what is being said about me even when I am being intimate with you and my husband. Kill the voice of the nay-sayers in my mind and heart. I need to be deafened to the voice of the enemy because every time I look at the situation the voice gets louder and louder and now, I hear them laughing at me. Father help me live in the truth of what I will birth. That all of your answers to me are yes & amen. Father, I need strength because discouragement has stolen to many moments of manifestation from me. Father, I am willing to carry this baby to full-term, birth it, and then give it back to you as a sacrifice for my "YES".

My friend, your prayers must become so involved that it will even change your outward appearance to those who are spectating. You must be willing to be misclassified as being drunk, delirious, or even giving a heavenly Oscar winning performance. It is ok. You just know and be willing to fight for your "yes" in the spirit.

A *Life Postured In Prayer* isn't just for you, it's for others as well. All the above-referenced people we discussed in this chapter fought in the spirit for a "yes" and denied themselves just so heaven could be released on earth for God's glory!

Remember, your "Yes" is unstoppable! The question becomes, how far are you willing to go in prayer to see it manifest?

YOUR "YES" HAS BEEN RELEASED, NOW SHOUT "AMEN" TO SEAL IT!

"YES"

An affirmative answer or decision; used as a function word to express assent or agreement

Walk In Authority

Our Authority!

The greatest gift, the greatest advantage, the greatest position of the believer, is our authority. Our authority is the bane of the devil's existence. Hell is absolutely disgusted with the authority of the believer. I did not say churchgoer, I said the believer. The greatest joy of the devil are the moments he is able to convince a born-again believer they are powerless against him; when in actuality, he is shaking in his boots hoping we never get revelation knowledge of our God "given" authority.

Confession: This is where I must continue to practice patience with my brothers and sisters. You may say, "what do you mean? You don't have patience with others?" Sure, I do. I am a Pastor. Let me explain.

The very first thing we are introduced to as believers is, "Authority". Here is what I mean. The moment we open our bibles and we get pass the table of contents, any explanations, and the forward the first book is Genesis. In the book of Genesis, in the 1ˢᵗ Chapter he releases a revelation that is absolutely life changing. Genesis 1:26-28 (amplified) states *"²⁶ **Then God said, "Let Us (Father, Son, Holy Spirit) make man in Our image, according to Our likeness [not physical, but a spiritual personality and moral likeness]; and let them have complete authority over the fish of the sea, the birds of the air, the cattle, and over the entire earth, and over everything that creeps and crawls on the earth." ²⁷ So God created man in His own image, in the image and likeness of God He created him; male and female He created them. ²⁸ And God blessed them [granting them certain authority] and said to them,***

"Be fruitful, multiply, and fill the earth, and subjugate it [putting it under your power]; and rule over (dominate) the fish of the sea, the birds of the air, and every living thing that moves upon the earth."

The thing I love is, God did not take us five books into the bible or even five chapters into the bible before he revealed to us "Our Authority". He put it front and center. 1ˢᵗ chapter, 1ˢᵗ book. To me that is significant. Before He gave us lessons on money, the blood, faith, friendship, manhood, womanhood, raising children, tithes and offering or the 5-fold ministry gifts; He gave us the premise of who we are and what we possess, "Authority". If you notice in Genesis, the 1ˢᵗ book of the bible, the enemy comes and test the "authority" that was given to man. He did not test their giving, manhood, womanhood nor their calling. He tested their "Authority". Listen at what he says in Genesis 3:1(NIV) *"Did God really say, "You must not eat from any tree in the garden?"*
I want to look at the words he used **"you must not"**, he was implying, you mean to tell me, you have been giving all this stuff, but this one thing "you have no authority" over. The first thing the enemy did was challenge their "Authority". This is what the enemy is saying to many of us today. He is saying "you mean to tell me with all the "Authority" being given over to you, you can't conqueror this or that? This is why I say, "I have to have patience" or the compassion of Christ, because I know the devil has no authority to question our "Authority". Yet he does daily. However, he does on a daily basis. A righteous indignation rises in me every time I see him questioned what has been given to us legally.

Let us talk a little more on the subject. The devil has a strategy he devised one time and he reuse it repeatedly hoping to get the same results he got on the day he approached Eve. That strategy is, he comes to put pressure on our authority. Do not come down hard on yourself if you have fallen to this one devise; so, have I. However, as my Christian roots grew deeper and my prayer life grew stronger, The Holy Spirit said to me, "Val it's his playbook and the plays haven't changed". I said, "got it"!

He tested the authority of Jesus many times, he did it to Abraham, he did it to Moses, he did it to David, he did it to Elijah and so on and so forth. His M.O. (mode of operation) is to challenge our authority. Why does the devil feel the need to apply pressure to our "Authority"? I will tell you why, because he knows if we get a full understanding (not just an understanding for the purpose of knowledge but an understanding for the purpose of use) of our "Authority" our prayers will always avail/produce much. "GLORY!!!"

For that reason, the enemy has devised another plan called pressure. He believes if the believer is overwhelmed by the pressures of life, they we will become too distracted to walk in their authority. He uses pressure to wear out the believer so that the believer will forget about his/her "Authority". With a sad heart, I admit too many beautiful believers have succumb to the pressures of the enemy and have forfeited their authority. This is how he defeats the believer on many occasions with insurmountable pressure, at least that is what he wants us to believe. However, according to the word spoken over and into man by God regarding our authority nothing is insurmountable. Why? Because we have been given the authority to subdue(subjugate).

What I have learned over the years as I have developed my prayer life/ prayer connection, the pressures of life are about one thing; they come to prevent our pressing into his presence with prayer and they come to blind us to our "Authority".

Lets' look at a great example to my statement above. Remember Jesus in the Garden of Gethsemane? That story is a perfect picture of pressure, pressing, and authority. The pressure of life(the cross was upon him, and not him upon the cross), the press was intense(prayer time) even to the degree he felt all alone in prayer, this is why he came back to those who were supposed to be in intercession with him and for him (Matthew 26:40) and said **(I'm gonna' Val'nize this interpretation)**... "Fellows I am not feeling you covering me, and **my authority** is being tested". I hear Jesus saying this in Matthew 26:40: "Yes this "pressure" is real, yes the "press" is real, but also my "Authority" is real. Fellows, you should have taken authority over your flesh". Remember, Jesus said "the flesh" is weak. In other words, you have "Authority" over the flesh.

This is where we see a vast number of believers failing to operate in authority, in the flesh. Unfortunately, this happens all the time in the body of Christ. I have often wonder what the missing link to walking in authority. Why is this so hard for the believer to grasp?

Why do some people fear walking in their authority? Or Why do some people reject walking in authority? Especially when it comes to the flesh.

Let me be perfectly clear, I have been down the road of fear and flesh and my authority was challenged to a great degree. One day I asked our dear friend The Holy Spirit about what fear does to one's authority. This is what He said, "the missing link is, when the believer doesn't find it necessary stay in constant communion with me" the flesh then usurps it's authority over a person's life. WOW! Ok, I can see that. He said "no, you don't understand". The word says "I, The Holy Spirit will lead you and guide you into all truths" and "I, The Holy Spirit will constantly remind you in all situations you have Authority" but when you are not in constant or regular communion with me the believer's ears began to grow dull to my promptings, my voice, and my reminding them constantly of their Authority".

Wow, Wow, Wow! I can see that. That makes so much sense. Jesus said in the word "I must go away, that the comforter may come". Jesus was not just referring to him as a comforter to those who you are sad, lonely, oppressed, etc... but he has come to comfort us and encourage us to "walk in our Authority". Praise God!

See, when we walk as we were designed to walk, how we were purposed to walk, then things that are out of order would immediately get back in order. Child of God, we must give credence to our "Authority" and stop treating the "Authority" given to us like some minuscule announcement given at creation. The Holy Spirit showed me it is actually an insult to our Father (The Most High) when we don't walk in our "Authority". Forgive us Father, In Jesus Name Amen!

When He declared he gave us "Authority" he put all of earth on notice; this man, made in my image and in my likeness is now ready to rule with all power and is ready to move heaven into the earth, with the words of his mouth, just like I have. My friend this makes the devil very uneased the devil is terrified of our "Authority". That's why prayer is so important, because prayer "gives" (give means: freely transfer the possession of something or someone; hand over to) us the "Authority" to transfer heaven to earth "FREELY" at any time. Glory!!!

My friend the devil does not want us to walk in our authority or pray from this place of "Authority". When we do, no-thing is withheld from us, especially those who understand who they are and the "Authority" they possess. When we pray with faith and do not doubt in our hearts, when we pray from a place of "Authority", heaven expeditiously move on our behalf. No wait times! I dare you to shout, "No Wait Time!" I truly could go on for another 7 chapters about this, but I must move on.

Ok, I cannot close this chapter out without pointing out something else. Prayer is a military term. The Holy Spirit said to me some years back "Prayer draws warfare". Well, I am here to tell you, so does your "Authority".

Listen what the word tells us in (Luke 10:19 NIV) _**19 I have given you authority to trample on snakes and scorpions and to overcome all the power of the enemy; nothing will harm you**_

This word "Authority" is a military term bestowed upon believers to serve notice to the enemy; this man I created in my likeness is fully "like" me. The "Authority" I have given him fully outranks your principalities, wickedness, darkness, imps, and strongholds and any other military forces of the enemy. Glory!!!

This one word "Authority" shuts the kingdom of darkness down. Therefore, the devil "does not" want you to know what you are operating in and who you are operating on behalf of. We are a part of the armies of heaven! The enemy is so terrified of this word "Authority" he devised a strategy to throw the believer off their game and that strategy is, pressure. With all diligence the enemy comes to wear you out by applying tremendous pressure to your life. He is predicating our demise on one thing, life-pressures. The devil has established his kingdom up on the foundation of applying "pressure" too you so you can shut your mouth from praying with and in "Authority".

I call "pressure" the garden of Gethsemane experience.

The enemy has developed the plan of pressure for one reason and one reason only, for you to forfeit your "Authority". The thing is, when we forfeit our authority, he cannot be held responsible by the courts of heaven for a right we forfeited. I leave you with this, when we forfeit our "Authority" we walk in the type of Esau. Esau forfeited his birthright(authority) all because he was tired, worn out, felt the pressure of his flesh desiring to be fulfilled immediately and he had not spent time with God to renew his strength. Do not let that be you.

Child of God, you have been given "Authority" so walk in it! Remember, no test, no disappointment, no press, no pressure is worth you surrendering your "Authority". So, stand bold, pray without ceasing & WALK IN YOUR "Authority!

Authority

the power to give orders, make decisions, and enforce obedience.

Victory In Jesus

Don't Downplay the Victory!

Our victory is what Jesus lived for, died for and is living for right now! It is always the desire of the Father and Jesus for us to walk in total victory. When you and I are declared victorious it brings the kingdom of God glory. When you and I pray, and results are manifested in the earth because we keep the faith in what we prayed, without wavering, it draws others closer to the kingdom and it displays we "don't downplay our Victory".

I heard someone say years ago "If Jesus has ever delivered you from one thing, you don't have a right to doubt him in anything". These words are totally a statement of truth. I think people tend to allow doubt to creep in their hearts because, we downplay our victories. In the bible, every time a battle was won the king that came out victorious never downplayed his victory. No, the king would throw a party and invite everyone to see his triumph. As believers we must let the world know about our triumphs. This is why I am a huge fan of testimonies because my triumphs in Jesus is worth sharing.

Have you ever thought to yourself, why is the devil so hell-bent on me doubting God? What does he get out of it? I tell you what he gets out of it, us doubting and downplaying past victories. He gets a chance to berate and belittle our faith before our father. That will never be his testimony about me to the Father.

I often wondered why people doubt a God that brought them through, brought them out, and brought them over numerous of times and they know He will do it again without hesitation.

Everything in our lives up unto this moment is a result of one of the above truths. We were brought through something, He brought us out something and He brought us over something. You may be saying, how do you know what He done for me? Well one thing I know is, Jesus delivered a "bring through, a brought out and a bring over when He died on the cross, defeated hell and set captives free, and when distributed VICTORY on the third day when he rose from that borrowed tomb! Let me point something out that shouts VICTORY in the word, "Borrowed Tomb". We buy things we plan to keep but we borrow things we plan to return.

Here is another confession for me, I have been a part of the doubting and downplaying crew as well until it was brought to my attention by The Holy Spirit, His Victory was for you.

One day in spending time with Holy Spirit preparing to write this book I heard him say, "People downplay their Victories" more than they celebrate their victories. Kind of shocked me because I tell everyone about my Victories in Jesus. The Holy Spirit told me when we downplay victories it is called "false humility". I was like what!? (as you can see, I love talking with Holy Spirit) He said "yes"; so, I pondered on that statement.

As a result of my meditating on that conversation I came to this conclusion. I believe people downplay their victories because in the body of Christ we have taken a worldly term "bragging" and translated it into the kingdom and replaced "testimony" with "bragging". (The devil is so cunning, argh) My apologies, I had a moment. So now when we release our victories it looks as if we are bragging but in actuality, we are "praising" and walking out the scripture in **Revelation 12:11.**(*NLT*) *And they have defeated him by the blood of the Lamb and by their testimony. And they did not love their lives so much that they were afraid to die.* I absolutely love that scripture. I want to hang out in that scripture for a moment and prayerfully what I reveal to you will cause you to never again downplay another "Victory". Listen we are given Victories to put heaven on display.

In the scripture referenced above you will see in the 17th word of that scripture it starts with, "They did not love their lives so much that they were afraid to die". The reason so many people downplay their victories is because their reputation and how others view them means mor to them then their "Victory" or defeating the devil. Everything the word of God ask us to do has significance. When our identities become more insignificant and heaven's identity becomes more significant to us, testimonies will be the norm and defeating the devil would be an everyday occurrence. Just like the devil is going before the throne daily accusing us of not walking in faith, nor using our authority, he also goes before the throne accusing us of "holding our testimonies hostage to our self-made identities".

Let's look at Paul and Silas' experience in that roman jail. (**Acts 16: 25-31 NLT**) *Around midnight Paul and Silas were praying and singing hymns to God, and the other prisoners were listening. 26 Suddenly, there was a massive earthquake, and the prison was shaken to its foundations. All the doors immediately flew open, and* *the chains of every prisoner fell off! 27 The jailer woke up to see the prison doors wide open. He assumed the prisoners had escaped, so he drew his sword to kill himself. 28 But Paul shouted to him, "Stop! Don't kill yourself! We are all here!" 29 The jailer called for lights and ran to the dungeon and fell down trembling before Paul and Silas. 30 Then he brought them out and asked, "Sirs, what must I do to be saved?" 31 They replied, "Believe in the Lord Jesus and you will be saved, along with everyone in your household."*

Ok, let us look at the importance of not downplaying our Victories. The bible tells us at midnight Paul and Silas started "praying" and "singing". My friend the moment they started to "sing" they were putting their "Victory" on display! The bible goes on to say that **the other prisoners were listening.** This represent people in the same position as Paul and Silas, but they were watching to see if their God would display heaven in the earth for these two guys. Paul and Silas praying and singing displayed confidence in their "VICTORY", God did not disappoint. (I'm going to Val'nize this for you). "Paul and Silas were communicating through song and prayer, keep watching a VICTORY is about to take place".

Let us look a little closer, we see the VICTORY happened and because they didn't downplay (sing quietly, worry about reputation) the VICTORY process, everyone in the prison was a partaker. My friend remember you and I cannot downplay our VICTORIES, why, because everyone around you becomes a partaker. I want to point something out to you. All because Paul had a life *Postured In Prayer* it caused a man to desire Jesus and his whole family became a part of the kingdom of God. "GLORY!" Remember, every time you downplay a kingdom victory you could be holding up someone's decision to make "Jesus The Lord" of their lives. Selah

As I close, I want to recap some of the reasons we should have our lives postured in prayer.

The first thing is, when we posture our life in prayer it is a statement that our strength, our dependence, and our relationship is anchored in/on El Elyon the MOST HIGH God. Our prayer life is a statement Jesus is top shelf in our lives. A life postured in prayer communicates to this world "I am in this world, but I am not of this world.

The second thing of why a life postured in prayer is so important and vital is because it communicates to this world your "Connection" to the real-life source. ***Deuteronomy 10:14 "To the Lord your God belong the heavens, even the highest heavens, the earth and everything in it."*** When we place ourselves in a posture to lend our spirit, soul (mind, will, and emotions) and body to hear from heaven then we are able to be change-agents in a world that desperately need change.

Which brings me to my third reason our lives should be postured in prayer. The bible tells us we are Ambassadors for the kingdom of God and an Ambassador does not live in a place of conformity. An Ambassador is sent to another country to represent the views, ideas, and governance of the country they represent.

The definition of ***Ambassador*** - a diplomatic agent of the highest rank accredited to a foreign government or sovereign as the resident representative of his or her own government: an authorized representative or messenger: a person who acts as representative or promoter of a specified activity.

How awesome is that? You and I are heaven's "Ambassadors" but if we are not hearing from our kingdom then we don't know how or what message to bring or represent in the earth.

Fourthly, when we posture our lives in prayer it gives us the courage and wisdom of how to walk in our God given authority. A life postured in prayer shows the enemy I know who gave me this "Authority" and I will not be like you(devil) and abuse the authority that was given to me out of love. Let me point something out here, Lucifer arrogantly chose his authority over his love for the Father. So, when you and I "posture our lives in prayer" it is us reminding him of something he forfeited for something he was given freely, that he no longer has, authority. When you and I pray and worship it drives him even madder because he no longer has that authority. Selah

Last but surely not least, our lives postured in prayer represent the "availeth spirit". What do I mean by availeth? Simple, I am talking about results. The bible tells us in *James 5:15-18 (NIV)*

¹⁵ And the prayer offered in faith will make the sick person well; the Lord will raise them up. If they have sinned, they will be forgiven. ¹⁶ Therefore confess your sins to each other and pray for each other so that you may be healed. The prayer of a righteous person is powerful and effective. ¹⁷ Elijah was a human being, even as we are. He prayed earnestly that it would not rain, and it did not rain on the land for three and a half years. [18] Again he prayed, and the heavens gave rain, and the earth produced its crops.

My friend, a life "Postured in Prayer" has been deemed to get results in the earth realm. "Hallelujah!"

As I close my time with you, I pray that your time spent downloading this book in your spirit has challenged you to bathe, soak, and posture your life in prayer.

I will tell you this, one of the greatest moves/decisions I have made in this lifetime is to surrender my life to prayer.

"I LOVE MY LIFE'S POSTURE", which is "PRAYER"!

Join Me, Pastor Val